SELF-COACHING MASTERY

Meet Your Higher Self

and Win the Battle Within

You are worthy of the life of your dreams!

♡ Jamie

JAMIE DOOLEY

www.jamiedooley.com

ISBN: 9781091105805

DEDICATION

To my clients, past and future, who continue to teach me about the beauty of human potential through imperfect action and sheer belief.

And to my family, for their love and understanding as I navigate across my fears toward a life of joyous allowing.

SELF-COACHING MASTERY SERIES
Book 1-Meet Your Higher Self

CONTENTS

INTRODUCTION

1	Clear your mind………………………………………………..	1
2	Let go of the past …………………………………………..	13
3	Becoming centered ……………………………………………	21
4	What don't you want? …………………………………….…	27
5	What do you want? ……………………………………………	33
6	A glimmer of authenticity ……………………………………..	45
7	Self-coaching basics…………………………………….............	55
8	Mastering your thoughts ………………………………………	65
9	Controlling your emotions …………………………………………..	74
10	How to take inspired action …………………………………….	79
11	What to do when you get stuck …………………………………	85

FOREWORD

This book, and especially this foreword, are a first of its kind. In it, you will learn powerful tools to help you bridge the computer system of your brain, which we are labeling the subconscious (SC), and your heart, which we call your higher self (HS). Mastery is about using your heart to program your brain. You can control your thoughts much like you steer a car. You are the driver, not the car. The car gets you where you want to go. Where do your thoughts get you?

I am so proud of Jamie for being brave enough to share the method that has worked for her with the masses. She was worried she would sound crazy. I've been tugging at her heart strings for decades, telling her she

...is enough

...has enough

...does enough

...knows enough

to share this message.

Within these pages is her secret to self-coaching, and stories from her life when I was calling to her. When she listened, she experienced outrageous joy. When she didn't, she felt confused and alone.

No one could teach her these methods, like I could. She learned them by going within. That is where we met. That is where she named me.

Your higher self is calling to you too. Will you listen?

Much love xoxo, Michelle

INTRODUCTION

Hi friend! I'm glad you're here! Something in you must have connected with this cover, or title, so I'm guessing that you, too, feel the battle that exists inside of you. I am humbled to be a small part of your journey within, and want you to know that YOU matter. YOUR STORY matters. The question is…Who is writing it—your heart or your brain?

Nothing I am going to tell you is new. I have spent 20 years learning from so many spiritual gurus, psychology and philosophy professors, life coaches, and self-help authors, that to claim any of this as *mine* would be absurd. Some of my favorite mentors have been song writers, who seem to say more, eloquently, with fewer words. I admire that. I struggle to finish most books, so each book in this series will be short and focused, to give you time to digest what you learn and put it into practice. We learn by doing, not reading.

In these pages I introduce to you my method for separating what goes on in my heart and in my head. There is no official research to back me up, and I am not claiming to be an expert on the subconscious in any way. I use the term to describe the computer-like parts of our brain, and the programs always running in the background. I always forget to clear the apps on my phone and my battery dies…super symbolic for life, don't you think? Our human creations mimic our lives and give us pointers to so much going on in our deeper selves. I wrote this mostly as Michelle, because I was too afraid of judgement and comparison. My words come from my heart, not a degree.

I was my very first client 20 years ago. A voice from deep inside said, "You cannot do this alone. I am here. We got this." Michelle may be God, my soul, my intuition, or divine essence. Either way, she speaks from my heart. Self-coaching is evolving. As more of us practice it, new tools will emerge. Mastery isn't about reaching the upper most level, it is about realizing you never will—but you move toward it *anyway*. My stories are meant to inspire you to take a look at where your old programs are running your battery down and making you feel defeated. The only battle you can ever win is the one within, and you do so by changing your thoughts. If I was able to, anyone can.

1 CLEAR YOUR MIND

"You have power over your mind—not outside events.
Realize this, and you will find strength."
Marcus Aurelius

I love research. When anyone asks me a question I can't answer, I excitedly pull out my phone to ask Google. I did some research for an online course I created a few years back and found a general consensus that we have approximately 60,000 thoughts per day. What's crazy is that of those, 95% are the exact same as the previous day, and 80% of those are negative (National Science Foundation).

I am not surprised. My inner chatter has always been relentless for keeping score of my mistakes, remembering useless details, and making me feel worried about ridiculous events that are so improbable, I should make movies about them. I can effortlessly whip up a whole storyboard of chaos to worry about instead of working on my to do list. And then, since the to do list never gets done, my chance at bringing something new into the world takes a back seat. Like back of the bus. My favorite flavor of self-sabotage is

"all the stuff I have to get done today."
I create the list myself, knowing I won't finish it, so that I can suffer more tomorrow with overwhelm and disappointment.

It's ridiculous.

It actually makes me laugh at myself…or is that Michelle laughing? It is getting harder and harder to tell us apart.

I had a pretty vanilla upbringing. Super small town, little crime, parents were married, friends and fun galore! I went to Catholic school, but didn't feel like I "knew" God. I could access Jesus easy enough through visualizing time with him, so that felt ok. What I didn't realize then, was that I wasn't allowing God to work in my life. I prayed when I needed something. I gave the directions. I was in charge, not open to fully receive.

The self-coaching concepts I am going to teach you came to me during traumatic events. I don't have to go into all of the details of those moments to explain to you how I got through them. No doubt, if you've been living longer than 20 years, you've felt your own inner voice, or knowing, pulling at your heart strings during some difficult times.

Some days it says, "What the hell are you doing?"

Other days it says, "It wasn't your fault, you didn't know or understand enough to avoid that."

During a tragedy, it just keeps you calm saying, "Everything is going to be ok." It may even help you separate yourself from your body for a moment until an event is over.

That small still voice is your Higher Self (HS). I use my middle name to label mine, since she is still me. Michelle is not other than me, just a specific part of me. The part that is pure love and light. The part that always knows what is right for me, and doesn't worry about what is right for others. She is my heart. She is always there, 24/7, and is a lot of fun to be with. Michelle can be thought of in many ways, depending on what I am going through and how I need her—mother, child, mentor, friend, soul-mate, spirit guide, inner voice, future self, or even God.

Regardless of what nick name we give my youngest daughter Jocelyn, it doesn't change who she is. JoJo, Pookie Junior, Peanut, and Jo all describe the essence of Jocelyn. I think of God in the same way. None of us have it 100% right. We can't. We are using human labels to describe that which is indescribable. That is they mystery of faith, and the definition. We must believe without seeing.

In this book, I will use the words God and Universe interchangeably. Feel free to think of any name you prefer. Self-coaching works for anyone, regardless of religion. Everyone has a heart, and everyone has a brain. It is about separating those two so that you can teach them to get along and work together for your common good. The tools I have learned support my faith, rather than compete with it.

People want validation that their words, and views, are the "correct" one, but as long as we don't hurt another, shouldn't we be more concerned with figuring out what is right for us, instead of what is right for everyone? I've been hearing the term Universal Human lately, and I like the idea. If everyone was diligently focused on improving themselves and their own lives, we wouldn't have much to argue about. I wasted a lot of time "helping" and judging others to be more like me. I should have been focused on my own voyage.

Mirror Effect

One of the hardest lessons I learned during this journey of self-discovery has been that when I am annoyed with someone for their words, energy, or actions, God is calling me to take a look at myself. I call it the "Mirror Effect." You cannot change other people. You can only change yourself. When you feel rage, tightness in your chest, or annoyance at someone else, it is a calling to look for that trait in yourself. I can tell you from direct experience (that still happens weekly to me), the lesson is meant for you. It's about you, and your growth. Other people show you, via the mirror effect, where you are ready to evolve and shed what no longer serves you.

Think of it this way, when someone says, "You can't do that." What they mean is, "I can't do that." You've heard that statement before, right? It's so true. We see everything in our outer world through the lens of our past experience, while filtering the data with our current programming and belief systems. We can only ever truly understand something from our perspective. So, when you notice something annoying in another, it is a call from your HS to adjust YOUR sails.

Any amount of time spent doing these things is simple avoidance of looking at your own self in the mirror:
- Trying to get another person to see your side (they aren't you, so they won't be able to, even if they say they can)
- Explaining how someone's actions made you feel (take ownership of your feelings and stop letting other people have that much power over you)
- Analyzing why another person may have done something (I don't know why I do half of what I do, so why would I be able to figure out someone else's actions???)
- Thinking about ways to get another person to change (manipulation)

- Explaining another person's issues to them and giving solutions they didn't ask for (forced life coaching)
- Problem solving for other people (unwelcome life coaching)
- Fighting, arguing, disagreeing, criticizing, and pointing out how your way is superior to other people's way (of course it is…for YOU in YOUR life…let others figure out what is best for them in their life)

Here is the cool thing; when you learn how to self-adjust, instead of trying to get someone else to adjust, you will notice the other person doing what annoyed you less and less. When we change what we focus on, the things we focus on change. If I look for what I don't like, I will find it. Same goes for the opposite. Happiness is a choice we make when we get up in the morning to make the most of what we have, put a positive spin on it, and be open to more of it.

I heard a story about a woman who yelled at her husband every day to pick his socks up off the floor and put them in the hamper. They fought about this every morning for 25 years. He died at age 50 suddenly due to a heart attack. The next morning all she longed for was to see his socks on the floor next to the hamper. Joy is not about your circumstances, it comes from your perspective, which you control with your thoughts. Be thankful to have a husband to pick up after. Be thankful to have a daughter to shuttle around. Be grateful to have a paycheck, regardless of the work.

The Pendulum

There is dichotomy in all things. Two sides. Two perspectives. And when it comes to relationships, two stories—constantly being written from past wounding, in a protective type of dance. To fully understand one side, you must also know the other.

For a pendulum to swing all the way to it's highest point on the right, it must also swing that far on the left. For us to know light, we must also know darkness. Part of what keeps us living the same day over and over again is the fear of the unknown, or opposite. The fear of failure. The fear of going through something. So we try to go around it, and fail anyway, because through is the only way. Don't fear failure. Embrace all the parts of the journey. Learn the lessons and enjoy the swing to the other side.

If I didn't grow up in Upper Michigan, I would not appreciate summer like I do. If I didn't have two failed marriages, I wouldn't appreciate my husband and our healthy marriage like I do. If I didn't know what being broke feels like, I wouldn't appreciate financial stability like I do.

Noticing what you *don't* want is the quickest path to figuring out what you *do* want. It's part of the process, so embrace it. You WILL fail. You WILL suck when you start something new. Contrast is part of everyday life. Use what you learn, and keep going. Don't get stuck.

Your Higher Self

In order to meet your higher self, all you need is some alone time. I do a "Future You" meditation often with my clients where I guide them to visualize a room where they will meet him or her. I've coached hundreds of people, and not one single time has anyone said anything bad about their future self! They are always happy, healthy, making more money, smiling, in love, etc… Which leads me to believe that it may be our fears and worry preventing all of this beautiful stuff from actually happening. We aren't receiving it.

We block it with our thoughts, which become our feelings, which program our actions and give us a less than desirable result—

Cognitive Behavior Therapy (CBT) 101.

To access this center of you, fully in alignment with God and the power of the Universe, you must go within. You cannot find your HS by reading books, taking courses, or absorbing anything from the outside world. That is why it is called self-coaching. YOU HAVE TO DO IT YOURSELF. This is a solo voyage. There is no one to blame if things don't turn out like you hoped, but you. Your beliefs matter more than your circumstances, and you are the only one who can change them.

Ouch! Don't believe me? How does placebo effect work then? Sheer belief. What about the fact that before 1954, it was a common belief that a human being could not run a mile in under four minutes. People who had tried failed. It was "common knowledge" like the world is flat. Once Roger Bannister proved us wrong, over 1,000 runners have done the same.

The impossible is now the *goal*.

Take a look at your own life. I sure have changed my beliefs over the years. A belief is just a thought we keep thinking. Because of it, our brain is programmed to validate it through what we notice. So who is the programmer? YOU. Your brain doesn't create, it stores and manages. Your heart creates. You create your own reality with your thoughts.

That level of ownership changes lives. It causes immediate and profound authenticity to emerge. To become who you are meant to be, you must first unbecome who you are not.

For the sake of this book we are going to focus on only one journey …YOURS.

Imagine the sea as life, and a sailboat as your subconscious. You still need someone to direct the sails. You are that captain. A sailboat needs wind and water to go anywhere, so don't fear the waves. They are teaching you what you need to learn to complete your journey. Sailing can be hard alone. Good thing you have a partner—your higher self.

The Universe is pouring a constant stream of wellbeing into your life at all times. You access it first and foremost with your thoughts. Joyce Meyer said once in a sermon I was watching, "We are so free we can choose bondage!" Boy, did that hit home.

Anything separate from God is fear-based. You do not need to be religious to understand or access the love available to you. You don't have to choose a box to fit into. What if individuality is the whole point of coming into a body? What if faith is meant to be as unique as our fingerprints? What if unconditional love is the highest expression of emotion and alignment with our Source? If so, many of us are in trouble because love and forgiveness of self can be the hardest to practice. I know lots of religious people who are hard on themselves. How are they supposed to love others when they don't even love themselves?

This LOVE is surrounding you and attempting to pour into your experience RIGHT NOW. The key is to be in alignment with it energetically. We are energy. We are creating and attracting with our vibration at all times, but faith is needed to allow it. You have to believe without seeing, and intentionally open up to it in your heart.

Based on your upbringing, it may be a challenge to erase past programming. However, just like you can upgrade Windows on your computer every few years, you can also upgrade your thought patterns.

Wellness Room Meditation

Meditation is an excellent way to clear your mind. I think of prayer as asking God a question, and meditation as listening for his answer. Others use it as a way to clear the chatter and be present in the moment. There is no special position or clothing needed. You do not have to spend an hour, take a class, or do anything specific.

The purpose is to be mindful, of the chatter. To notice the difference between you (your HS) and your subconscious (the chatter) that we will from here on out call SC.

Listen to it, and clear it. Again. Again. Again. Catch yourself and watch as your mind wanders away with nonsense. Be the viewer. Don't judge yourself. Just observe. Breathe. Set an intention to focus on your breath. Clear more thoughts. Set the timer for 5 minutes. Work up to 15 minutes and do it when you wake up each day. Focus on feeling good. Visualize good stuff happening to you in the future. You don't have to wait to have something before you can feel good.

You can feel good NOW!

This good feeling place is where you can start to hear the whispers of your heart. This is where your HS may speak to you.

Take a moment to record the bold below in your own voice on your phone, or look for my version on YouTube. Speak slowly. Then sit or lay and play it back with your eyes closed. Allow this guided visualization to show you the love present for you if you can clear your mind long enough to feel it:

Take a big cleansing breath. In for two…out for three…

Again, in for two…out for three…

Imagine yourself walking down a hallway that never ends. Everything is white—the floors, walls, doors, and trim. It is brilliant and feels clean and shiny. Keep walking…

There are so many doors. Feel the freedom of being able to choose one.

Feel the peace of being free to walk as long as you like…

When you see a door that interests you, maybe it is your favorite color, or a door you recognize, open it.

Inside is your ideal cozy setting. Feel the warmth of the room. Maybe there is a fire going. Or maybe it is spring and the windows are cracked, letting in the smell of fresh cut grass. Notice your favorite flowers in a vase. You feel safe here. You feel protected, and loved.

There are two chairs facing each other. Sit in one. Imagine all of the healing power of this room starting to meld with you. Let go…let it all in…surrender to it healing anything that ails you.

Fear, uncertainty, and doubt cannot exist in this room. It is protected by God. Feel your heart turning to pure GREEN energy. Let it fill your entire body. Feel it in every cell.

Now let it expand 1 foot beyond your body…
And then, if it feels ok, pour out and fill the room…

The whole room should be filled with shiny, silky, vibrant, green heart energy.

Soak this up as long as you like.

When you feel recharged and rejuvenated, ask your higher self to come sit across from you. Honor whoever shows up for you as correct for you at this time. Ask if they have a name. Ask if they have a message.

This is your Wellness Room. Stay here as long as you desire. When you open your eyes you will be back in your life, with a new sense of centeredness, peace, and appreciation for all you have. Any negativity you were feeling is healed. You are pure and whole. This is a fresh start to your amazing life...WELCOME BACK!

Believe it or not, this recorded visualization is less than three minutes long. In only three minutes, at any time of the day, and anywhere, with only your cell phone, you can CLEAR YOUR MIND and center yourself.

We tend to self-sabotage by saying "I would, but" many times a day. Think about all of the things you say you would like to pursue or have, but do not have the time, money, or knowledge. Lots right?

Watch for the phrase, "When I have _____, I will feel _____." That is a slippery slope preventing you from feeling that emotion. You have to change that thought. But first, learn to clear your mind. Close all the open tabs running in your SC.

2 CLEAR THE PAST

The Stories We Tell

"But" is a dirty word that I removed from my vocabulary many years ago. I used it the most often during a disagreement with my significant other, now my husband. It protected me. It helped me prove my side…or so I thought.

All it did was make him feel misunderstood. My ego thought that my side of the story was right, and therefore worthy of his validation. The lesson I learned was that I was right, and so was he.

We were both living in different stories!

Neither of us could know the history of past hurt, trauma, disappointment, and despair present in our hearts at that moment. Neither of us could fully understand the triggers or "thorns" being rubbed against because we had not lived each other's story. We still believed we WERE our story, and that the voices we heard telling us we were right were helping us. I now know they were needlessly protecting us. Keeping the thorn in place. Preventing us from doing a re-write.

"There is nothing more important to true growth than realizing you are not the voice of the mind – you are the one who hears it." Michael Singer, **The Untethered Soul**

This simple, eloquent statement is so vital to you understanding the rest of this book, that you may get tired of me saying it. I will paraphrase it many times in this book and future books in the series so that you can find what sticks to your ribs.

YOU ARE NOT YOUR THOUGHTS.

YOU ARE THE THINKER OF YOUR THOUGHTS.

Mr. Singer's book single-handedly changed my life. I had been living in a reactionary state, protecting my wounded child (and wounded adult) from all matter of things, for 36 years. Even though I had a very positive outlook and attitude at work, and in the public eye, I was quite miserable inside.

Looking back, I can see the problems as stepping stones to where I am now. Each breakdown of my story provided me a new perspective and another chance to take control of my thoughts so that they didn't control me. Until I read his book in 2011, I believed that other people were responsible for my happiness.

Because I believed I was contributing to their state of happiness by fervently and obsessively taking care of them in ways they never asked me to.

Whoa…

It was a shocker! Suddenly all the things other people did to annoy me had nothing at all to do with them, and everything to do with my fears about my "ideal" not coming true. I believed my story and picture of the future was so vital to my happiness, that it absolutely must be what they desire too?

No.

Not even a little bit.

By learning where my thorns were, and removing them one by one, new avenues for healing and understanding opened up for me. I found the book *The 5 Love Languages* by Gary Chapman, and suddenly understood why no one else in my home ever cared if the house was clean or the dishes were done. Acts of Service wasn't their love language, it was mine!

> (If you haven't already taken the 5 Love Languages quiz, hop on over to www.5lovelanguages.com and do it now. Gary Chapman helped my family communicate at a higher level, and I recommend everyone take it to understand themselves better.)

I read everything I could get my hands on by Brene Brown, and finally understood that my perfectionism was keeping me from vulnerability and therefore true connection with others.

I apologized to people. Sometimes verbally, sometimes just silently in my head and heart. I asked my sister, Lisa Freitag, an amazing health coach who had just started to do deep emotional work with clients, to help me cut some cords.

I'll never forget when she said, "There are tools to your right, what do you think you need to cut this cord?" and the answer was a chainsaw! I had no idea the ties that were binding me to my story…and the thoughts that were keeping me re-writing it, over and over, year after year, relationship after relationship, to validate my narrative.

Finally, and most recently, I learned that you can only love another to the extent you love yourself. With all of these undesirable programs running in the background, my battery was on 2%. With my specific love language (and flavor of self-sabotage), I believed that if I worked hard enough for those I loved, they would respond in kind and charge me back up. They did! But with *their* love language.

I got hugs, and jewelry, and small handmade gifts. And more laundry, shoes to put away, and dirty dishes. I now clean my house because it is important to ME. I now provide myself with my love language. I understand that the love I want to flow to my family, friends and clients' needs to flow over from my self-love stash. I can only imagine what my life would be like if I would have understood that earlier. BUT (let's use it in a good way), I would not be able to connect with others on this imperfect journey if I didn't have those experiences.

Control over your mind and your thoughts should be the most important goal of every day. The to-do list will get done, only for more stuff to get added to it tomorrow. To control your mind, you first have to get good at being aware of what is going on up there, and then be able to clear it. Imagine it as your cell phone. Double click and close all those running apps (old programs) that are draining your battery.

Taking Control

Change is hard, unless we believe it is easy. My clients hate when I remind them they are the only person who can change their story. We are human and we like for others to "take our side" and tell us it isn't our fault. Will Smith gave one of my favorite YouTube speeches of all time, "Fault Vs Responsibility,"

> "It don't matter who's fault it is that something is broken, if it's your responsibility to fix it. For example, it's not somebody's fault if their father was an abusive alcoholic. But it's for damn sure their responsibility to figure out how to try to deal with those traumas and make a life out of it. It's not your fault if your partner cheated and ruined your marriage, but it is for damn sure your responsibility to figure out how to take that pain and how to overcome that and build a happy life

for yourself…Your heart, your life, your happiness is your responsibility and your responsibility alone. As long as we are pointing the finger and stuck in who's fault something is, we're jammed and trapped in victim mode. When you are in victim mode, you are stuck in suffering. The road to power is in taking responsibility. Your heart. Your life. Your happiness, is your responsibility, and your responsibility alone."

No matter what tragedy you have lived, what grief or loss you feel the weight of, or what trauma you have in your past, your choice to heal is the most powerful decision you can make.

You can play the victim for the rest of your life, but no one will suffer more than you.

During the free call I offer to see if I am a good fit with a client, they often ask "how" to heal. The answer is so easy that it almost sounds sarcastic. Make the decision to, and let go. That's it. No amount of thinking about, analyzing, or obsessing about the past is going to change it. You cannot heal by fixing it in your mind. It is unfixable. Stop beating yourself (and whoever else was back there with you) up. Give yourself permission to move forward.

LET IT FREAKING GO.

Don't tell anyone about your decision, unless you are working with a coach. Coaches are not emotionally involved (or at least they shouldn't be). They just guide you toward the next step by helping you connect with your inner knowing. Your "loved ones," God bless them, are emotionally invested in your story and the roles they play. They *do* have an agenda. They are trying to prevent their thorns from being bumped and are in process of writing their narrative of their pain, and their justification for it too. You are a player in their story and they may not like it if you change characters on them suddenly.

They will not be objective, and it doesn't matter if they support you anyway. You are doing this for you. Any spillover of happiness into your outer world will be bonus points.

Don't go into work and announce that you are letting your anger toward your ex-husband go while another staff member is just beginning her divorce process after listening to you complain for a year, and may feel "abandoned" by you.

Don't call your mom and tell her you've decided to stop holding her responsible for the family falling apart right before a holiday get together either.

As you will see as we continue, this has nothing to do with them. Your healing is your responsibility. Just let go, and stand outside of yourself. "Watch" yourself from a third person perspective. Sometimes Michelle stands back with me and says, "Watch what Jamie does here…she says this a lot…it stems from a situation that happened when she was 12, remember?"

Self-coaching requires a ton of self-awareness. Taking yourself out of the equation can prevent you from getting pulled into the emotion of it, and just be objective.

Most of what we fear never happens. The number one fear humans have is public speaking, yet no one has ever died from it. Watch your fears and worry play out. See how you re-write the same story over and over.

Ask yourself what you could do different here next time?

Ask yourself what someone who doesn't have trauma in their backstory would say?

Ask yourself how you could help this relationship improve by changing your patterns?

To your surprise, there will not be fireworks. The person you forgive will not even know…proving to you that you were the only one suffering this whole time.

When life feels hard, ask yourself what your HS thinks or feels? He or she is pure love and light and does not hold on to lower feeling energy. Remember, if you'd like to meet yours, ask them to be in your Wellness room next time you visit. Imagine 2 chairs and invite them to sit in the other facing you. Many of my clients see their HS as their future self. Honor your process, faith, beliefs and visions. This isn't about me teaching you what "works." Every single author thinks they have it figured out because they figured out what worked for them. By sharing what worked for me, I hope to inspire you to figure out what works for you. If something else comes up during your meditation, try it.

Exercise

Many people find it helpful to mark this moment with a ceremony. Seeing your past go up in flames is powerful.

Write down everything you regret, wish you could change, wish hadn't happened, are ready to let go of, or no longer serves you. It may be a failed relationship, financial distress, career failure, extra weight, clutter in your home, negative self-talk…anything that holds you down or back.

BURN IT. You now have a new foundation to build your ideal life on. You have solid ground again!

3 BECOMING CENTERED

"The highest levels of performance come to people who are centered, intuitive, creative, and reflective – people who know how to see a problem as an opportunity."
Deepak Chopra

We discussed being centered in Chapter 1, but making centeredness part of your daily essence is the key to success in self-coaching. Many people call it being mindful or present. All good things flow from this place of calm, peaceful, self-love.

Remember the analogy about the sea? You cannot get to the peaceful part of the sea without the waves to get you there, but you cannot be objective if you are fighting six foot waves either. When the water calms, everything is clear. Learn to calm the water before making decisions. Use that Wellness Room meditation to fill whatever room you are in with peaceful, green, heart energy. Then watch how people react to you!

My First Time

When I first started playing around with my heart energy and its effect on others, I was still a clinical dental hygienist. I was already in school to complete my bachelor degree and move into administration, but was still working full time at a dental office. I was in physical pain every day. I wasn't making the money I needed as a single mom, so I started life coaching on the side. Patients asked to meet me between appointments and they bought me coffee and often gave me my hourly rate as a hygienist, which is all I asked for. They couldn't do much talking while I cleaned their teeth, so at these in between meetings, I did a lot of listening. I found out I was a good listener, and asked good questions.

I had so many patients who I loved…and a few names I dreaded to see in my schedule.

One sunny summer day, Mr. G we will call him, came into my operatory with an extra attitude. He raised his voice, told me he HATED seeing me, and didn't know why in the hell he had to come every three months. He said, "GET THIS OVER WITH! HURRY UP THIS TIME!"

I got all worked up and teary. I told him I needed a different instrument and left the room to dry my eyes under my safety glasses. I ran to the bathroom, closed the door, leaned against it, and started to cry. I said under my breath, "I hate this fucking job!"

As if Michelle was in there with me, I heard in my heart, "You will stay at this job until you change your attitude. It isn't the pay. It isn't the patients. It isn't the pain you are in. Your attitude is the problem. Change it."

Shit.

I knew she was right.

I closed my eyes, visited my Wellness Room, and filled that bathroom with as much green heart energy as I could muster. I went back to Mr. G, sat down (remember, when you go to the dentist your head is literally at our heart level) and worked. We did not speak. I sent him more love than he had probably ever felt before. I oozed it. When I was done, I asked him which day he'd like to return for his next appointment and he said, "Young lady, I don't care as long as it is with you. I am sorry about what I said earlier. I've had a rough year. You have a gift. I felt so relaxed and enjoyed this time with you very much. Do you ever meet people for coffee?"

WHAT???

It freaking worked! That was the day I learned I can have an profound, immediate effect on others with my beliefs and energy. Since that day I've practiced it by phone, many states and time zones away, with the same success. Mr. G showed me that what I was really meant to do was coach, and that the most important part of coaching was for me to be aligned with that reservoir of love instead of giving advice, lecturing, or teaching anything.

And--it gets better--I received two nonprofit internship invites later that week, so I never saw him again. I left that position and started a new journey. There were a few more bumps in the road, but I learned that very day what being centered was, and how it could positively affect my life, and the lives of others.

I saw my problem as an opportunity to grow and improve that day. I shifted the blame from Mr. G to myself. It started me down a completely new path, one of authenticity. Once I realized the power my thoughts and emotions had over my experiences, I started to dream bigger than just what I thought I might be able to make a living doing. I envisioned my purpose being bigger than one patient at a time.

That employer told us at a meeting once, "The good ones never stay." My coworkers and I blinked hard at each other, feeling like chopped meat. What did that mean about us? He was right though. Growth and expansion are inevitable. If you aren't changing, you are falling behind.

The Power of One Thing

One of the best ways to get centered is to have one goal you are working on at a time. I used to be proud of all the stuff I could juggle, until I realized I was just spreading myself thin, and settling for lower quality in all areas. There is only so much of us to go around. Think of yourself as this picture below. Just being awake and digesting food and running your organs takes battery life. Sleeping takes battery life. Your SC is draining just doing the auto-pilot stuff, which makes up most of your thoughts and hours already! If you are going to have the energy to create something new in your life, you need to let a few other areas go. There is no such thing as being a good multi-tasker. You just give each task less of your excellence.

Pick one thing to focus on at a time. When you wake up each morning, get centered then ask yourself, "What one thing is most important today?"

Make it something you REALLY want. Here are some questions to get you started:

What is something you keep saying you want to do, but don't?

What would be worth running your battery down?

What would help you replenish your battery?

How can you fill your own cup today?

What would your future-self thank you for doing?

What is your HS calling you to do today?

One of the mistakes I see people make is trying to lose weight (diet), get in shape (work out), create a new income stream (start a business), and redecorate (shopping) all at the same time. I can tell you from first hand experience, you will fail. The failure is built into this self-sabotage story. Then you have an excuse for NOT getting results. Focus on one thing at a time. If it's large, like writing a book or creating a course, reserve hours in your schedule just like you would an appointment with someone else. The appointments you make with you should be your most important.

There are only so many bars on your battery life.

Women, especially, come to me tired. They want to know what is wrong with them. Why does life seem so overwhelming? They believe they need better time management to improve their lives. I often hear, "I just need to get organized." Nope! That is going to keep you disorganized. To feel organized, you need to change your words to, "I am organized." This small shift has changed my life.

- Think it *before* you have it
- Feel it *before* it's real
- Think and feel it *into* existence
- Smile *until* you are happy, not *because* you are happy

Your beliefs are more important than your circumstances. A belief is just a thought you keep thinking. Your outer world is nothing more than a byproduct of your past thoughts, that led you to feel a certain way, and then act or *not* act, based on how you were feeling, to validate your belief. It's a closed circuit, on repeat. Your heart is the only one who can reprogram it.

Most of us don't even know what we believe until we are asked, which is why coaching is so effective in breaking down barriers to success. To self-coach, you have to be the thinker and the listener. You have to realize your beliefs can hold you back or set you free.

Your HS will help you figure out the difference, but writing a new program takes energy. Which is easier, opening an old file on your laptop, or creating a new one? Your SC has access to all those old files and likes to be busy, so in the absence of direction, it will open all those tabs for you and keep them running in the background. Being centered is like closing them all, and opening just ONE. Deliberately choose just one that REALLY matters right now in this moment. Then watch your life change.

4 YOU GET WHAT YOU FOCUS ON

"Whether you think you can, or can't,
you are right."
Henry Ford

Everything starts with a decision. The ability to make one is so important when creating change in your life. And, NOT making one is still making one, so you might as well take a risk and move toward something.

When you wake up each day, what is the first thought that enters your mind? Is it dread? Is it whining? Or is it gratitude for another day to love your children, see your friends, and have an impact?

Do you spend time thankful for all you have, or do you mumble at not winning the lottery yet?

You get more of what you focus on. It has been said that there is only one topic—two ends of the same stick, what you want and the absence of it—but that they are still the same stick.

Basic Law of Attraction states that we are energy and that like attracts like. I used to think talk like this was Woo Woo. Then I saw the movie "What The Bleep Do We Know?"

Back then it was pretty cool CGI. I re-watched it recently and enjoyed the review. It was cutting edge for its time. Science and physics were supporting spiritual mystery in a type of merging that I wasn't taught in school or at church. I love research and scientific proof, especially when it backs up faith and the unseen. It taught me to appreciate the power of thought and belief and to question what I considered reality for the first time.

In the Zeno Effect, atoms will not move while you watch. I learned that on Big Bang Theory and looked it up. It's true!

The power of positive thinking has support in medical journals. In one study in 2007, Korean researchers found a strong connection with positive thinking and overall life satisfaction.

Neurologists in London have discovered that people who visualize a better future are more likely to bring that future to fruition. If LOA is new to you, read more at www.lawofattraction.com.

Regardless of whether or not you fully understand HOW the energy flows from a light switch to a lamp, doesn't matter, it still happens. You don't need to understand how LOA works, but honor your process. There is plenty of information to review online! I believe it supports my faith, versus contrasts it.

Another way of explaining this is that if you "Change the way you look at things, the things you look at change." Dr Wayne Dyer taught me so much prior to his passing. He taught me to be kind and gentle to myself. As a huge perfectionist, that had been a challenge. He had a very unique way of viewing his world and did not fit into any one box. I've always felt like a middle man too. I can always see both sides, which I used to view as a curse, but now I see it's been a blessing for me. I can bridge two things that don't seem to have one.

I am a good intermediary. I crave balance and appreciate both ends of the stick for what it shows me. I like the swinging pendulum.

He got some backlash for it, but he also taught me not to worry about what others think of me. If I help one person when I create, it is worth any backlash from those who don't agree with me.

What Do You NOT Want?

A great starting point to what you want is what you don't want. That is pretty easy for most people to define. The problem is getting stuck there. I call it "Analysis Paralysis."

Our lives get so busy that we can tend to live on repeat. My sister always says that "We don't live 100 years, we live the same year 100 times." So sad, and so true.

Whether you like it or not, thinking about what you don't want, don't like, or are tired of, does nothing but give you more of it.

You get what you focus on.

If you are new to this theory, try to think about red lights on your way to work and watch how many you hit. Think of a number in your head over and over and watch it flood into your life in the form of a bill, radio station, license plate, etc…

Enough Money

Let's use money to go a little deeper into this topic. It can be confusing, especially when self-coaching, to take apart why thinking about money rarely leads to more money. It seems to be in direct contrast with my statement of "You get what you focus on," right?

When I coach, I have some low months. It often seems like feast or famine. Everyone has experienced a flood of work or business then a dry spell. But how are they connected?

My vibe attracts my tribe. When I have enough money and time, my vibe is high. I am in the habit of having *enough* clients and *enough* money, so I have an ABUNDANCE MINDSET. My thoughts aren't on money because I've already been paid. I am not blocking more from coming in. My thoughts are on helping my clients achieve results. I am in the flow.

People want to work with me. People want to be around me. They want what I've got. I get referrals from those people. I talk at seminars and get a few *more* people to sign up for private coaching and then I stop promoting myself because I have "enough" clients. Then I feel a bit overwhelmed. I pull back…I don't want *too many* clients. This is *enough*.

Toward the end of those three months, I may realize that I don't have many, or any, new clients starting to take their place. I am feeling the LACK of money. I am self-promoting with a LACK MINDSET of "I don't have enough money, wanna be my client?"

See the difference? My results have nothing to do with the pool of clients available to me, and everything to do with my thoughts. If Michelle is in charge, my thoughts are positive, and I am not blocking *enough* money. If my SC is in charge, my thoughts tend to be worry based, and I don't have *enough* money.

You get what you focus on. Thoughts become things.

Enough money is the same wording. The difference is in my vibration. It is in how I am feeling. The emotion of it all programs the energy I put out into the world. My circumstances haven't changed. There are tens of thousands of people on social media that are interested in my coaching services. My thoughts of having enough money, or needing enough money programs my emotions, which leads me to act in certain ways, and gives me an outcome.

My feelings trump everything else.

So the purpose of my asking you to write what you want down in words is so that you can see it, tangibly, objectively, outside of yourself, and then think about the emotion attached to it.

When you read those words, how do you feel?

If it is a LACK emotion, you won't get it. If you think or feel "yeah right!" or "Must be nice," you are feeling the opposite of what you want.

If it is an ABUNDANCE emotion, you will get your desire.

You have to fully believe it is possible, and feel REALLY GOOD thinking about it, without any worry about *how*.

How is not your job. That belongs to the Universe. Your HS knows how to get you there, one step at a time. You have to trust him or her enough to fully surrender your desires and feel the feelings NOW, versus wait.

You can learn to hack into your SC to reprogram it to think positive thoughts. Writing helps to activate the deeper programming. When you write down what you WANT, your SC looks for ways that may be true. If it's true, taking action seems like the next logical step. What you focus on changes.

Exercise

Take out a piece of paper and write a line down the center. On the left write "Don't want." On the right write "Do want."

After centering, set the timer for 5 minutes. Empty your brain and allow whatever shows up to get written down.

Don't worry about the how.

That isn't your job, it's God's.

The more "don't wants" you have, the more negativity you are focusing on in your life. Move them over to the other side by rewording them to "do wants.

5 WHAT DO YOU WANT?

"When you practice unbending intent, you match up with the intent of the all-creative universal mind. So, keep a solid picture of the task you want to accomplish in your mind, and refuse to let that intention disappear."

Dr. Wayne Dyer

Intention is the back story for creativity. Many people call it "finding your why." I stopped advertising my coaching as a service to help people with their why because I don't believe we are limited to one!

My first why for leaving my 15-year career was because I needed greater flexibility for my daughter's needs and I was tired of wearing scrubs. During the 2.5 years I was getting my Bachelor's degree it became the fact that I was in daily pain and was starting to drop my instruments…luckily always on the floor instead of down someone's throat.

Over time my why has shifted to more freedom, benefits, autonomy, passion, and the sheer number of people I want to help. Why isn't singular. Those searching for just one are stuck in self-sabotage. Pick something you'd like to have and move toward it. Don't read one book and think you're stuck because what worked for the author isn't working for you. Self-coaching is about trying out many methods to see what helps you have your own A-ha moments, and break the chains that have been holding you back from living a life you love.

So, what do you want?

When you come home from work and the kids have made a mess and dishes are piled up and your fight with your significant other is still fresh in your mind, it's easy to know what you don't want.

Studies show we want feelings not things. Harvard professor Gerald Zaltman says that 95% of our purchasing decisions are subconscious (Inc.com). He says his study concludes that emotion is what really drives purchasing behaviors, and decision making in general.

It makes sense if you think about it. Do you want a red convertible to park in the garage, or do you want the feeling of driving on the open road at 60 mph, with the "wind through your hair" kind of freedom that item provides?

Do you want to be debt-free on paper, or do you want the satisfaction of knowing your hard work paid off and you can now feel confident when bills come each month because there aren't many and you know you can pay them?

We want feelings.

And since feelings aren't permanent, what we want is bound to change as well.

Subconscious Mind

Change happens in our subconscious (SC). I like the way Brian Tracy, a top sales coach, says it on his blog, Personal Success. Here is the gist of his explanation:

It is like a huge memory bank that stores and sorts nearly everything that has ever happened to you. Its job is to store and retrieve data. It helps you respond exactly the way you are programmed to, based on your concept of self. You can reprogram your own thought patterns by slipping in new sound bites. By focusing on uplifting ideas, your SC will begin to implement a positive pattern in your way of thinking.

Your conscious mind can be thought of as a garden, where the seeds grow if it is fertile soil. Your SC mind works day and night to make your emotionalized thoughts, hopes, and desires come through as behavior (or action). Your SC mind grows weeds or flowers, whichever you plant.

It also has homeostatic impulses and manages your autonomic nervous system. It keeps your heart beating and lungs breathing without effort. It keeps your mind on auto pilot as well, making sure you think and act in a manner consistent with your past. It knows your comfort zone and works to keep you there ("*Subconscious Mind Power Explained*" www.briantracy.com).

Part of being a Master at self-coaching is understanding the difference between our comfort zone and growth. We are programmed for safety. Our genetics haven't changed much since we needed to run from saber tooth tigers. If you have access to this book, you likely have your basic needs taken care of, and are in no physical danger, but your SC is still programmed to keep you safe, and living small. It actually believes that change leads to death. It says to you, "Because you didn't die yesterday, let's do EXACTLY that again, ok?"

Thank God you are the thinker of your thoughts!

By making a decision to change your thoughts, you begin to control them, instead of them controlling you.

When people talk about "consciousness expanding" on this planet, that is what they mean. We have the time, knowledge, and resources (largely due to the information age), to download a new program by our understanding.

Brian Tracy is also a huge supporter of written goal setting, like me. He teaches the SMART goal technique. I created the STAMP method from that technique that I learned in the public health setting writing grants. Both of us believe that regularly writing your goals helps you make productivity and growth part of your comfort zone.

You can actually become comfortable being uncomfortable!

When you attempt to do something new or different, fear or resistance to change will show up. That is 100% normal. It means your SC is working. The good news is that when you stand outside of yourself in this moment, as your HS, and observe the outdated pattern, you can intentionally shift it. Each time your HS overrides your SC, your program gets an update. I also think of my SC as my human self (body and brain), and my HS as my spirit self, or soul. When they are all living in harmony, life feels good. When I ignore my HS, Jamie can be hard to live with—even for me! Being in touch with Michelle, and letting her speak through the whispers of my heart on a daily basis helps me stay centered and moving forward. It also helps me feel outrageous joy in the moment for all I have. Michelle is pure positive energy. She is always living in the present. She only speaks and feels love, joy, freedom, and appreciation. I know I am connected to her when I feel *good*.

Being in harmony also helps me to focus on the outcome I desire, as if it's already happened, which is why I changed the SMART process to include emotion. Our thoughts lead to our emotions, but our feelings can also be indicators of what thoughts need changing.

Successful people regularly push themselves past their comfort zones. I always try to be "just one step" outside of mine. If I take two steps, I run back to safety at the first sign of that saber tooth tiger who may now be a bully who makes a fake social media account to tell me I suck as a writer and I'm ugly (true story). *One* step out means I can easily get back to safety quickly if needed.

So what do you want to plant?

Many years ago, I created a system to start reprogramming my SC. I called it "Monitoring My Internal Landscape." I don't know if I read about it or created it myself. It's been said that people don't own information, just the organization of it.

My way of organizing what I want, versus what I don't want, is to imagine a garden in my head. A shrub or ornamental tree is the big stuff, like family, home, career. The flowers are hobbies, and fun. Each time I have a negative thought, and I (The Thinker of the Thought or Higher Self) notice myself watering it with my awareness, I visualize plucking it, and replacing it with a fresh seed—something beautiful instead.

I spent a lot of time preparing my garden when I first noticed how negative my mind could be. As my girls got older, I even created their own gardens, separate from mine, and groom those for them now. They overlap in certain areas, but I know at some point they will be fully responsible for their own growth. Now that they are older and out in the world as independent young women, I have to pluck more weeds than ever. When I start to worry, I plant a white lily.

I know I have an effect on others because of the Mr. G story. Could it be that our faith and worry can cause things to grow in other people's gardens? I'm not sure, but if I use the guidance Michelle gave me that I am on track when I feel good, worry is not helping anyone.

Plant and prune only what you want to grow. Pluck what you don't want to grow. "Water the seeds, pluck the weeds."

My STAMP Method

Once you get good at catching yourself having a thought that doesn't serve you, you can learn to replace it with a new thought, or mantra. Once you have better control over your garden, you are ready to use written goal setting to hold yourself accountable for the life you are constantly manifesting. You are now aware that in the absence of a "boss," your SC will take over. Once you give your HS the reigns, the next logical step is to write your very own manifesto so that you have a map of where you are going. Remember, your thoughts are the vehicle. You are the driver.

By using my STAMP method, you will be joining the ranks of other Master Manifestors who have created and are now living their Ideal Life in six to 12 months. Use it to plan your next trip toward what you want. Where do you want to go?

In order to coach yourself, you need to get to know yourself at a deeper level. There can't be any bullshit in the way. No one needs to see your list but you. However, if you share it with at least one other person, studies show a much higher chance of success versus those who do not write their goals down or share them.

I call this manifesto writing, and I am an expert at it. I have now written seven personal manifestos that have come true. The only ideal that got moved to the next manifesto each time was "write a best seller," Through deep exploration, I realized I was afraid of being well known. Once I removed the phrase *best seller*, and changed it to "write a book that helps 10,000 people," it started to flow.

A "goal" can feel overwhelming and I am hard on myself if I don't achieve them. A manifesto is a kinder, gentler look at the space between where you are and where you'd like to go.

It is one tool in manifesting your ideal life.

It is one tool in self-coaching.

I created an online course on it a few years ago to find out if it would work for others in the same way it had worked for me. It did!

Many people were able to write down five to seven things they wanted, but didn't have yet, and accomplish them within approximately six to 12 months.

Writing forces clarity. It is a bridge between your SC and HS and helps tremendously with decision making. The exercise you did in the last chapter filters into your manifesto. Because I only gave you 5 minutes, your fears didn't have time to take over. We hijacked the SC to hear the whispers of your heart.

Growing up I often heard that "You can't help how you feel." I believed it, and therefore it was true for me.

After reading hundreds of self-help books, and developing this method, I now know that is not true.

Our thoughts lead to our emotions. Want to feel better? Think a better thought.

Here are some examples of "ideals" written using my STAMP

method on a manifesto:

"Now that I am a full-time, work from home life coach, I have unlimited income, freedom to put my family's needs first, and a sense of purpose helping others thrive by January 1, 2019." (buy new leisure wear to work in)

"I feel so fit and strong now that I am working out 3 times a week by May 1, 2018." (gym membership)

"Now that I have my ideal home, I feel a sense of peace and belonging by August 1, 2017." (house warming party)

Notice the feelings these people were after. By getting clear on what they really wanted, and being specific about the details, it was easy for them to come up with the next step in achieving their ideal.

My method is where law of attraction and science intersect. Writing activates your SC to look for things you didn't notice before because you were focusing on something else.

It also helps *you* hold *you* accountable for ACTION.

There is a story I heard in church once that always sticks with me. A man of great faith prays every day for 50 years to win the lotto. Day after day, he is faithful with his kindness, and love for all, and chores, and prayers. When he dies, he asks Jesus, "Why didn't you answer my prayer?" Jesus replies, "I tried to son, but you never bought a ticket."

What I found out in teaching written goal setting was that it only worked for people who:

1. Had faith enough to believe what they wanted was possible
2. Were willing to ACT, even if they failed because they believed they would learn something that got them closer to their goal
3. Were willing to take action that was uncomfortable
4. Understood what Inspired Action was

We will go into Inspired Action later, but we have already covered the other three.

If you aren't there yet, don't bother writing any goals. Work on being centered.

Faith is the foundation. You MUST believe what you want is possible, and you must believe that if you fail you will learn something valuable.

Belief in Action—JoJo

My youngest daughter is pretty much my mini-me. She is a Type A perfectionist who was born self-sufficient, mature, responsible, and independent. I cannot take credit. I don't feel like I teach her much. If anything, she teaches me.

There has been nothing she's put her mind to that hasn't worked out. I watch her tirelessly balance school with a 4.2 GPA, dance (and assistant teach dance) 18 hours a week, nanny part-time, help out at home, and have fun with friends. From time to time she gets a bit stressed. I will say, "Take a break peanut. Stay home. Take a day off. Rest."

Her response is typically, "No, I committed to this and myself. I can do this. I just have to stay focused."

Whoa...she's only 16!

Sure, she knows I believe in her and support her fully, but there comes a time that our beliefs and dreams for our kids may not be as powerful as their own. I've taught her that anything she desires is within reach and that all she needs to do is:

1. Believe it
2. Take action toward it

It is rare, but sometimes things don't turn out as well as she had hoped. That happens to all of us, right? So what defines those who succeed from those who give up?

The will to act, *until* they succeed.

Jocelyn is a competitive dancer. She started late, and is not naturally flexible. She has had to work twice as hard as many dancers, and watched team mates and friends do better than her at competitions—year, after year, after year.

Yet, she never once quit.

She never once gave less of herself…she gave MORE.

This year, I've seen tremendous growth! She is getting noticed—off stage, for her leadership skills, and work ethic. On stage—for her strength, passion, and storytelling. She is mentally, and physically, so strong. She is always chosen to lift others in routines, and her solo is scoring well. She has taught me one of my favorite mantras, "We rise by lifting others."

She wouldn't be where she is today without the adversity. If dance was smooth sailing for her, she'd be bored. The waves have made her who she is today.

Her team is amazing as well. They have spent the last few years being overlooked by the judges. They perform stories. They are unique. At the last competition we went to, there were studios with crazy technique and ability. They were like robots—nailing quadruple turns and tricks with ease. JoJo's instructors centered them as a group before going on. They were told to be present, and grateful that they get to do what they love. They had been given a story to perform, not dance moves. They scored the highest routine of the entire weekend and won 1st AND 2nd place. They believed in themselves, and danced from their hearts, instead of worrying about the outcome. They enjoyed the journey so much that the audience was pulled in. We felt what they felt. Many of us parents wept. Their emotion poured out into the entire room. We lived that story with them for three minutes. The judges were *moved*.

I felt nothing when the perfect robots performed.

Your emotions are guiding you toward the next step. Pay attention to what makes you feel good. What *moves* you? Figure out what makes you *unique*, not perfect. Then choreograph your dance. Share yourself with the world in a way that grabs people to *feel*.

Exercise: Write Your Own Manifesto

Take out a second piece of paper. Look at what you wrote in the DO want column.

Ask yourself if you believe it's possible?

> NOTE—You do NOT need to know HOW it is possible. Faith means you are allowing your higher power, higher self, God, the Universe, Source, and any other name you prefer to support you. Doing life alone has gotten you to where you are today. Only Massive Imperfect Action that is supported by faith and inspired by surrender will get you to the next phase.

If you believe you can have or achieve it within around 1 year use my STAMP method to get clear on the details. The Universe loves clarity.

Make sure it is measurable enough to know when you have it, and then build in a celebration in parenthesis. One of the main reasons clients come to me with burn out is they are really good at setting and achieving goals, but they do not take any time to celebrate them, they are already on to three more by the time they get the one they set last year.

Lastly, ask yourself, "If I had this fully, how would I feel?" That is really what you are chasing, the feeling, not the thing. By seeing that on paper, you can look for opportunities and memories that help you connect with those feelings NOW, instead of waiting to have the ideal.

That is where that first SPARK OF JOY lives…in knowing you can FEEL anything you desire, at any moment, with only the use of your thoughts. You don't have to wait to have a specific thing in your life to feel good. In fact, if you do, you'll be waiting a long time, because IT WORKS IN REVERSE!

You must feel good FIRST in order to have good things flow to you. You will attract them by being in alignment with them. You get more of what you think because what you are thinking is programming what you are focusing on. Your SC is always supporting your current story. It is always validating your perspective. It doesn't care whether your current story is positive or negative, it just sifts, stores, and retrieves data for you. Your HS is capable of feeling good RIGHT NOW.

Get centered, find something to feel good about (Can you walk? Can you hear?) then write as your HS. Imagine giving him or her the pen, and see what flows out. You now have a guidepost for decisions. If an opportunity is in alignment with your manifesto, do it! If it isn't, pass. And, like I tell all my clients, get ready because when you commit to something by putting it in writing, the Universe steps up to support you FAST.

6 A GLIMMER OF AUTHENTICITY

> *"You only are free when you realize you belong*
> *no place – you belong every place – no place at all.*
> *The price is high. The reward is great."*
> Maya Angelou

You will never be able to figure out who you are, what you want, or what your "why" is while looking to others for guidance. They can only help YOU understand who THEY are and how they got there.

The path to authenticity is lonely.

It's a road without pavement. There are no street lights, park benches, birds flying, or friends walking dogs. It is dusty, dark, and overgrown because you are the first one to have EVER travelled it, and you are the only one who ever will.

Reading self-help books, including this book will not teach you how to get there. All that learning from others does is teach you how they got there. Up to this point, I have shared MY story. This is what worked for me.

It has been decades of reading, listening, learning, fighting, loving, laughing, drinking, crying, sadness and joy.

Reading the work of others can both be inspiring and tricky at the same time because reading feels like action, but it's not.

Talking about books that inspire you feels like action, but it's not.

The type of action that will get you where you want to be has nothing to do with others, it is INWARD. Get comfortable with silence. Get comfortable being alone. Get to know all the parts of yourself. Have a meeting. Lay out the ugly stuff on the table and decide what to let go of.

Tell "everyone" that from now on only teamwork will be accepted.

I have found that my diet plays a big role in my personal development and creativity. Each time I have been able to create something that helps others, I have been eating in a way that does not cause blood sugar spikes or cravings.

I've gotten to know my body well through dancing, running, yoga, lifting, HIIT, and meditation. I now feel at home in it, and thankful for what it does for me.

I've also made peace with what I see in the mirror, but maybe that is just called "turning 40." I have learned to look in the mirror for something I like, versus something I don't like. I always notice what I like about other's appearance. It's easy for me to find something good about another's body. I notice great legs, beautiful eyes, gorgeous hair, or even a nice blouse on other people. My eyes look right past anything less than attractive to the MOST attractive parts.

Don't we deserve the same for ourselves? Negative self-talk is a bitch. Don't invite her to the party.

Authenticity is like opening a gift God gave you that no one can see but you. No one will understand it—they aren't supposed to.

The crazy thing is that I spent so much time trying to fit in somewhere that I made myself crazy! I wasn't like anyone else. You aren't either!

When you are 100% authentic, you are as unique as your fingerprint. There is no one to compete with, and all of a sudden, your life is beaming with other authentic people too.

Brene Brown says authenticity is the antidote for shame. I felt a lot of shame growing up, but I know it wasn't my circumstances because my sister and I have spent years on the phone taking apart feelings, thoughts, and memories to make sense out of ourselves and our limitations only to find out we remember every single event differently.

And we had the same parents, went to the same school, shared friends, were only 2 years apart, and shared a bedroom. Our circumstances were near identical!

Our perspective, and the part we played in our own narrative of what was going on, shaped who we are today.

Damn that SC.

If only I would have met Michelle earlier. Actually, I did, but my SC was so programmed to protect me that I paid more attention to my thoughts than my heart. Doubt can be a bitch too.

Belief in Action-Don

The person who has taught me the most about authenticity has been hands down my husband. He is 100% unique. I cannot think of a single other person like him. He doesn't shy away from being himself regardless of others opinions. If someone doesn't like him, great…one less person to have to manage.

It was hard when we first started dating. I thought I could help him blend in and be more politically correct. Turns out he was meant to help me.

I spent so many years trying to figure out what was "right" that what was authentic never had a chance at being entertained in my mind. I had no idea who I was or what my truth was. I just blended into the group I was with. I kept my beliefs in the background. I didn't really know them at all.

Through countless hours of drinking coffee together in the morning, and having deep discussions on all of life's mysteries, I saw the very first glimmer of myself. As I got triggered and didn't agree with him and his beliefs, I started to figure out what mine truly were. The craziest part was, when I saw the glimmer of my authenticity, the entire path leading up to it lit up magically before my eyes. My HS had been speaking to me all along. I just wasn't ready to listen. We both feared each other's differences, but our fears were unfounded. As we laid them out on the table, we could see we often felt exactly the same, but were using different words to describe our version of the story. When we broke down the wording differences, we could dissolve the fears together, one by one. I'm not saying it was easy, but man was it worth it!

Don also has a very successful career in sales. He has shown me belief in action. When your paycheck depends on the numbers for the week or month, and you are doing and saying all the right stuff, without the desired result, you have to get good at surrender.

He inspires me.

How To Embrace Your Authenticity

Like Maya Angelou said, you belong no place and every place, kind of at the same time. It that "both ends of the stick" analogy again. Dichotomy. To know light, you must know darkness. For a pendulum to have the power to swing far to the right, it must swing equally to the left.

To be able to coach yourself effectively, and become who you already are, you have to go through many uncomfortable phases, much like a butterfly who goes into a pure liquid state while in the cocoon. It literally digests itself, releasing enzymes to dissolve its own tissue.

Go on Three Dates with Your HS

1.   Unbecome who you are not.

On date one, stop pleasing others by playing the role they gave you in their narrative. BE YOURSELF. Take the time to get to know you. You pick the restaurant, you pick the wine, you stay out as long as you desire, and bring a journal for notes. See what spills out when you allow your HS to speak. Label the pages like this:

> 1.   What brings me joy:
>
> 2.   I feel prosperous when:
>
> 3.   In my ideal life I have:
>
> 4.   Things I love to do:

Getting to know yourself can be a lot of fun! It doesn't have to cost you a penny either. Take baths. Take walks.

If you found yourself living in a completely different city, where you didn't know anyone, and money was abundant, who would you be? What would you do to fill your days?

Trying to please others is a slippery slope. When we are little it is just mom. When we start school is it just our kindergarten teacher. Then more teachers, and friends, and cute boys, and pretty girls, and bosses, athletic coaches, and people you are friends with on Facebook that you've never met…it's dumb. Stop it.

You cannot be all things to all people.

2. Figure out what your victim story is, and re-write it

Like literally, take a bad memory, and flip it to remember it differently. I've done this with my own and my client's sexual trauma memories. It's powerful and helps you go from victim to victor in your life. It is a form of NLP. It works best with a professional, but since 90% of coaching is self-coaching (the space between the phone calls), you have to do the bulk of the work alone.

You cannot raise your vibration high enough to make lasting change while living in victim mode. That is a cop-out—remember Will's speech.

On date two ask your HS if there are any victim stories running in the background. The thought that comes to you in the first 1-2 seconds is correct. That is how you will know the answer is coming from him or her, versus your SC.

Michelle speaks to me quickly. She doesn't have to pull data from the filing cabinet of my brain. If I get stuck over thinking, I clear my mind, connect with Michelle, and have my answer in 1 second. I can even ask her questions and there is the answer, sitting in my heart, waiting to be heard.

Take what comes up and re-write it with you as the victor. If that seems too hard just play a supporting character in the story and make the bully or person at fault five years old. Do what it takes to run the movie in your mind with you having the power. Ask yourself:

1. What would this have gone like if we were both acting out of love?

2. What would have happened if the other person wasn't wounded?

3. What would have happened if I wasn't wounded?

4. What could make this day or story less powerful?

5. What would this memory look like if I had owned and used my personal power instead of giving it away?

6. How can I remember this event positively? What words or feelings can I omit or include?

I believed I had my personal power taken away when I was young, so I protected it by trying to control relationships. When I re-wrote the story, I realized that no one can take our power, we give it away. I gave mine away by NOT doing or saying anything when I was uncomfortable. In my new narrative, I used my voice to say what I was thinking and what I wanted to happen. I imagined being in control during that encounter. I wrote it the way it should have been. It healed me.

Hurt people hurt people. When you re-write your story, make sure to forgive all involved, including yourself.

3. Figure out what you want

On date three, you should know yourself much better, and be future focused versus pulled backward with shame or guilt. Now is the time to take out your manifesto and ask yourself why you don't already have those things? Where are your beliefs limiting you? What can you replace them with? Look for the times that you say:

If only I had more time.

If only I had more money.

If only I had a supportive spouse.

If only I could figure out what I want to do with the rest of my life.

"If only" belongs in the same category as "But." Catch yourself when you say it and rephrase it. Flip it to the opposite.

I have the time.

I have the money.

I have a supportive spouse.

Watch your language for the next week. Words have power! What words do you use on auto pilot that need to go?

Should is another word to stop. Don't do anything you "should" do anymore. Do what you WANT to do. Stop living according to someone else's ideals.

I've recently changed my ideal body from a specific number on a scale to the words "energetic" and "strong."

Take a social media break while doing this. I take Facebook off my phone when I'm going deeper within or creating something new. NO ONE NOTICES! My ego wants me to think my business will dry up and people will forget I exist. That never happens. A week off, or if you can do it a month off, will help you remember who you are and what *you* enjoy. Connect with real people outside of social media. Go to a coffee shop and strike up a conversation with a real LIVE person. Bring your journal to a park bench and connect with nature. Here are a few questions my sister asked me many years ago to help Michelle and I align. If you do no other writing exercises I suggest, answer these questions on the following pages:

1. **What would you do if you could not fail?**

2. **What mantra can help you get there?** (A mantra is a positive thought you "plant" when you catch yourself having a negative thought. It's the opposite of the weed.)

3. **What would someone who already has what you want be thinking or believing about the world around them?**

7 SELF-COACHING BASICS

> *"I am responsible for everything I think and feel.*
> *No one can cause an emotion inside of me."*
> Brooke Castillo

I have been coaching for a decade, sometimes dabbling, sometimes helping friends, and most recently as a real business. I doubted myself for a long time. People would tell me they thought I was gifted in some way, but I always blew them off. No doubt, you've experienced the same. Stuff that comes easy to us seems "too easy" to make money doing.

A few generations ago, you had to physically work hard for money. You even had to physically work hard to make and slice bread and churn butter for the week. That isn't the case anymore.

Now that life is easier with technology, and better systems and processes in place, we can focus on new areas of growth. My background is in starting programs and businesses, so I love the idea of continuous quality improvement, or CQI, in work *and* life!

Never before in history have we been so interested in, or in touch with, how we are feeling.

We have expendable income and expendable time, due to all that CQI. We are paying $5 a day for coffee, $12 a day for lunch, and a couple hundred dollars each month to keep our "healthy" wine habit flourishing. We scroll the same newsfeed on our phones hours per day. We live in a first world country for sure.

Moving the self-help crusade along has been the booming coaching industry, which is currently the second fastest growing profession in the United States, beat out only by Information Technology.

After half a century using money to buy things, we have begun to realize that things do not bring happiness. If they did, rich people would all be joyous and content. People are starting to utilize personal coaches, and coaching methods, to help them find the self-limiting thoughts they are caught in so that they can consciously create a new loop that makes them feel *good*.

We are understanding, at an astounding rate, that happiness is a decision you make when you wake up each morning to be happy with whatever you currently have. That takes new programming. We cannot get new results with the same thinking that got us the old result.

Self-coaching has risen from the desire to hold ourselves accountable for our own personal development and happiness, while spending as little money as possible. People now see the value of coaching, and since so much info is out there about it, they are finding more and more ways to get started on a dime. Since 90% of coaching is self-coaching, it makes sense to get as far as you can alone on your sailboat, then hire a professional if you get stuck. There are some things you cannot see on your own.

Gratitude plays a huge role in staying centered enough to experience growth and change. You cannot feel good and bad at the same time. Something will tip the scale. Remember, your results aren't based on your circumstances, they are based on your feelings. To get good feelings, you need to think good thoughts.

The mantra I created for myself, and live by, is "The quickest path to what I want, is gratitude for all I have."

When life isn't moving as fast as I'd like it to (which happens a lot for me), I deal with it by feeling satisfied and appreciative of the now. I look around at all the things I wanted once, and now have, and I get in the zone of *wanting them still.*

You can still want something after you have it.

Raising my vibration to that of appreciation attracts more beautiful, freedom-affirming situations, people, and vibes into my life. Whether you use the LOA or "thoughts lead to action" model here, they both work. They are cut from the same cloth, but use different wording.

When we are authentic, we are as unique as our fingerprints. Authentic people really like themselves. They don't put much, if any, stock in what others think. They get centered and listen to their HS.

We can all use different words to explain or understand the same concepts. The wording is less important that the emotion or vibration. Feelings are what we are chasing, but they are not in a place we can ever buy or catch them, they are free, and they are within.

Moving Away From Being Reactionary

In my online manifesto writing course, I taught people how to move from being reactive to proactive. It is a simple shift, that can be incredibly difficult to master. When you get good at it in certain areas of life, like at your job, there is always another layer. Another level to reach…like a video game. This is book one in a series of self-coaching titles because I felt that many short books would be easier to digest and implement than one giant, long book.

We are always co-creating with our HS, and Michelle and I have been arguing over the series idea for the past two weeks. I've lost countless hours of sleep as she builds me up and tells me why I can do this. My SC has argued for all of the reasons I cannot. It brought up every fail all the way back to my childhood, then all of the people who will say "Who does she think she is? She sure as shit doesn't have it all figured out!" They are right, I don't. No one does. Since you are reading this, obviously Michelle won.

When we are proactive we are creating, or manifesting, our reality INTENTIONALLY. We are always creating our own reality, whether we are aware of it or not, so setting the intention of what we want to have is powerful for creating our best life.

I found The Life Coach School and Brooke Castillo a few weeks ago when doing research for this series. I wanted to see what else had been published using the term self-coaching. I loved the way she put circumstances at the top of the coaching model I was taught in my CBT and life coach certification trainings. It helps people self-coach in a way I haven't seen before because it is a simple visual. All you need is a napkin and a pen.

> Disclaimer: It is always the most beneficial to use a professional coach trained to guide you toward uncovering your true self. It can also be good to have a supportive person there during what can be a very emotionally draining and trying time. Realizing you have created your life experience to date with your thoughts, fears, beliefs, emotions, and eventually, actions or nonactions, is hard to swallow at first. With support, it can become exhilarating to realize that ownership brings with it power for change, and beauty, that was not possible before. You were too busy blaming other people and looking to preserve your story before. Transformation takes energy.

With that said, Brooke's explanation and model are helping people get started without the expense of a coach. If you are super self-aware, and the beginning of this book was more like review for you, you may have great success. She has an abundance of free videos on YouTube and a book called *Self-Coaching 101* if you'd like to go deeper. She covers every topic you can think of and gives great examples. I am going to order it as soon as I finish writing this!

Here is the gist of it:

Circumstances

Thoughts

Feelings

Actions

Result

I often write the middle three on a piece of paper and help the client see the loop they are stuck in, so that they can figure out what they'd like to feel instead. I've been told that my asking "What would you like to feel instead?" sticks with people, long after we work together. When our SC is running the show, we become reactionary and forget we can choose!

Brooke helps clients self-coach by showing them the difference between their circumstances and their thoughts.

We cannot control our circumstances, which include other people.

When we are stuck saying "If only," we are blaming our circumstances for our lack of desired result, instead of our thoughts about the situation. The result then further validates that the thought was correct, true, or real. In reality, only the circumstance is factual. It is neither good or bad. The thought about the circumstance is where we put a spin on it with our perspective.

So *The Life Coach School* basic self-coaching model would look something like this:

Circumstance (fact)—I weigh 135lbs

Thought—I am fat

Feeling—Depressed/Tired

Action—Lay on couch and eat a bag of chips

Result—Gain more weight

I wish I weighed 135lbs. This is a real example from a client! See how the result is simply further programming to keep you in the loop, thinking and feeling the same things, taking the same action (or non-action) to validate that you were right all along?

We trick ourselves to think that since we cannot change our circumstances (this person is still going to weigh 135lbs today, regardless of the thought), we cannot change period.

We say, "A-ha! I knew I was right. I knew this would happen. My life sucks. Why bother?"

Brooke teaches that our thoughts are not necessarily true, but an interpretation of our circumstances. Like I said earlier, it's about perspective.

If we take this same model, and clear it out, here is how a private session with me would go with this person:

Me "So you feel depressed and tired. What would you like to feel instead?"

Client "Not depressed and fat"

Me "Ok, I see that you are so far into this story, that you are having a hard time believing anything else is possible for you, right?"

Client "Yeah, I guess so."

Me "What is the opposite of fat and depressed to you?"

Client "Skinny and happy, but those are too far of a stretch."

Me "Ok, what feels possible to you that is just a little better than how you feel now?"

Client "I don't know."

See how stuck in this loop we can get? Her fact, thought, and emotion are so wrapped up in each other she believes they are all unchangeable. She has probably tried in the past and failed, leading her to believe that diet and exercise don't work and are a waste of her time. Her belief is what needs to be changed, not her circumstance.

I am not sure how other coaches would approach this situation, but I would help the client see that the thought "I am fat" was the self-limiting belief that was becoming a self-fulfilling prophecy.

The cure is to change the thought to something believable. I would work with the client to find that. Sometimes it takes multiple calls and exercises (homework I assign) to get them there.

In this situation, I would ask what this person's ideal weight was, and what someone who weighs that may be thinking day to day. The answer is likely, "Today is a good day, I look great, I love kale, I love going to the gym."

We would take apart how true these statements are and pick one for them to use for the next week. For instance, "I Look Great." By saying that many times a day, and visualizing their ideal body at their ideal weight, the SC can be activated and will literally start looking for ways that is true and step up to support it.

By waking up and thinking "I look great" you are more likely to groom yourself, take the stairs, go salsa dancing on Friday night, and eat foods that nourish you. Being negative supports NOT taking care of yourself because you're not worth it, and it's not worth it.

That is the seed we talked about earlier. Weeds will grow if you don't plant and water what you want instead.

Mel Robbins teaches us the science behind this software. Our brains have a Reticular Activating System (RAS) that filters certain information to come through, and blocks other info. Who programs this complicated network of neurons? You, and the people from your past.

If you feel unlovable, your RAS will look for ways that is true. If you feel like people don't like you at work, it will confirm that for you all day long, due to something called Confirmation Bias, where we like to hear and read things we agree with, to confirm our filter. If your brain let in everything, it would cause your computer to crash. It's just too much info. Media is coming at us from every angle all day long. Input. Input. Input. We need the filter.

The good news is that you CAN reprogram your RAS, with self-coaching tools such as writing down your goals and visualizing them as if they've already happened, like we discussed in Chapter 5.

Imagine a great big symphony; a group of talented musicians all gathering to play music together, but the director doesn't give them any sheet music. Their job is to play music, so they will all play from memory whatever they can remember. It will sound horrible. Your mind just plays from memory as well. It is more like a parrot than a songwriter.

Your HS is the song writer. Give your musicians the same sheet music. Write down what you want so that your band can play in harmony.

Balance out your manifesto by having something in each area of life: relationships, self-care, health, home, career, fun/vacations. A symphony of only strings will not sound as rich as one with strings, percussion, horns, and woodwinds.

Balance your life intentionally. Your life is your symphony. You get to write a new one as often as you desire!

There are other coaching models to explore and I will go deeper into them in future books. This series is meant to inspire you to learn from other coaches and teachers too, not just me. Motivational interviewing, neuro linguistic programming, hypnotherapy, emotional freedom technique, and cognitive behavioral therapy are all popular methods in both the psychology and coaching worlds that I have had success with.

Explore them, and see what jumps out at you. Again, reading what works for me, or any person or coach, is only a starting point. Self-coaching is like deep sea diving. Practice in shallow water first. Figure out how much you can do alone, then find someone to take you deeper.

You have to do the work. The inside work. You have to get to know yourself and your bullshit, by digging all the way to rock bottom. Once you find ground zero, there is nowhere to go but up. As you rebuild, and realize no one can captain your sailboat but you, you can learn to use the sails to go anywhere you desire.

You know you are pointed in the right direction if you feel good. If you don't, adjust your sails.

8 MASTERING YOUR THOUGHTS

"The only limits in life are those we impose on ourselves."

Bob Proctor

So here you are, you've learned so much and done the writing exercises and read more books and visited more websites, and listened to Abraham Hicks, Bob Proctor, and Napoleon Hill on YouTube, and you don't see any evidence of change.

You are exactly where you are supposed to be. You are on the journey. You are in the middle of the ocean. You are in process. Don't let the speed of it make you second guess your direction and get you off course. Keep your sails pointed as planned. Enjoy the ride!

To become an expert at something, you need to study and practice 10,000 hours. That breaks down to around four hours a day for seven years. I am an expert at self-coaching because I have been diligently pruning my thoughts for the past eight years. Mastery is different. A true master knows the craft is constant. Each peeled back layer reveals a new one. There is no such thing as done, perfect, or the end. The journey you have embarked will last the rest of your life. Learn to use the waves and enjoy the calm in-between. Relish in the view!

My bestie and I were talking the other night about how planning vacations is as fun as the trip itself. If you've ever had a trip that didn't go well, the planning stage may have been the best part! Deciding where to do, asking people for their favorite stops, creating the schedule, buying the tickets, booking the hotel or VRBO, shopping for clothes, getting in shape and tan, talking about it with the people you are traveling with....yada yada yada

People sail for the point of sailing. They return to the same place they started from. They go out on the water to enjoy the journey. It's the whole point. Stop trying to get your manifestations to come true so fast. Milk it!

Learning all this mindset stuff is the easy part. Putting it into practice when the stress of day to day life hits is what can be hard, at first. After a little while you remember that since you don't have to wait to feel what you want to feel, you already have what you want. You get there by going within. Get centered and raise your vibes (which is all sight, sound, and emotion are anyway-look it up!).

When the outside world isn't changing, it is likely because you are focused more on what is, than where the sails are bringing you. Anyone on their death bed will tell you that they wish they could do the journey part again. They want the feeling part, not the owning part. No one says I wish I still had a red convertible sitting in my garage. They want to experience the freedom it provides, barreling down the highway with the top down, radio up, smiling and laughing. The car is literally the vehicle to the emotion.

When you get frustrated, focus on the feeling you want. Feel it now. Remember a time you felt that way, or imagine how you think it will feel. Visit your Wellness Room from Chapter 1. Do anything it takes to get you in a place of feeling good. Give to others. Get your focus off of you. Volunteer. Help those less fortunate.

Someone, somewhere is dreaming of the exact life you have right now. They would trade places with you in a heartbeat. Find something to be grateful for. Leave your house. Be with others. When you are feeling low, one of the worst things you can do is sit home alone with your thoughts. A belief is a thought you keep thinking. If your thoughts aren't positive, your SC is running the show. Ask your HS to take over. Surrender. Your beliefs matter more than the facts or circumstances. That is where your power lies.

You are in control of your thoughts. You are the only one. Roll up your sleeves and pluck some weeds.

Belief in Action—Zoe

My silver lining mentality stems from raising my oldest daughter, who has spina bifida (SB). She was the first person to teach me what perseverance looks like, and she was only 2. She inspires everyone she comes in contact with. My girls have been two of my greatest teachers.

Even though Zoe is a paraplegic, she walks unaided. She is pretty much paralyzed below the knee, along with bladder and bowel. Growing up was hard for her at times, but now at nearly 20 years old she attends college for accounting, lives alone in a dorm, and has a boyfriend. I did not know God or my HS very well before I had her, but I was damn sure going to need to align with them to give her the best chance at a quality life. I minimize her special needs, but at one point she had 14 different healthcare providers! It's a lot to manage and organize. It was like a part time job. If I wasn't a healthcare provider myself who understood so much of what was going on, it would have been much harder. I learned to practice gratitude for whatever was going good.

- One of the reasons your thoughts are still popping weeds may be that you have not surrendered to the powers that be.

I am a type A control freak. It was going to take a BIG challenge for me to lean on God and the Universe, and I've had more than one. Each failure has taught me to appreciate my imperfections instead of try to hide them. I now view them as blessings.

I never told Zoe what she couldn't do. I tried my best to focus on what she COULD do, and gave the rest to God. I surrendered. I am now teaching her to surrender. I often remind her how good she was at it when she was 8:

We were moving and she was going into 3rd grade. She had worn her leg braces her whole life. She didn't walk until age 2 ½ and it took a surgery and countless hours of physical therapy, bracing, and a walker. She asked me if she could start her new school without leg braces. She wanted to be like the rest of the kids.

I took her to her orthopedic surgeon, Dr. H, who has since passed away. He was a dear man, a gentle soul, who was a patient at my dental office and loved to go to Zumba classes at age 70. He was a man of great faith. He let her walk up and down the hall with and without them and said under his breath, "Let her go the summer without them. Her legs will tire, she won't keep up, and she will want to wear them again. Don't tell her she has to though."

She happily put them in her closet, believing she didn't need them anymore. We made vision boards that Saturday and she put a pair of legs on there. They were just regular legs, like a razor add. She went to bed.

The next morning, I woke her up so she could catheterize. She was rubbing her eyes and groggily said, "Is he still here?"

I said, "Who?"

She said, "Jesus. He was in my room all night staring at me. He was so tall his head went through the ceiling so he kind of had to lean over. It was weird."

Whether you are a Christian or not, whether you believe this was just a dream or not, that little beauty never wore those damn leg braces again. We weren't even attending a church at that time.

I brought her back to Dr. H at the end of summer like requested. He watched her walk up and down that hall unaided, strong, proud, and with grace. Through teary eyes he leaned over and whispered to me again, "Well I'll be. I had a feeling it might work. She just needed to believe in herself. Mom too."

I still get chills thinking about it today—our beliefs matter more than our circumstances!

When I was pregnant, Zoe's dad (my then husband) and I received a high AFP reading which meant there was a chance of spina bifida, twins, down syndrome, or wrong due date. The next step was to have a 3D ultrasound an hour away to get a better look at the baby. Since we were trying to conceive due to my endometriosis, we weren't planning on doing any testing to find out if there were problems, because we knew we wouldn't terminate. My mom was watching the Today show and saw a story on Vanderbilt. She called me to say she just felt like we needed to go through with the 3D ultrasound. If it was spina bifida, we could do this in-utero surgery, or at the very least have a scheduled c-section so that the sack of nerves outside her back did not shred coming through the birth canal.

I said fine to appease her, but wasn't worried. If I haven't already said it, listen to your mom. Mine has always been right. Even when I don't like what she has to say, she has an innate intuition that astounds me. My mother must know her HS quite well!

Sure enough, there was the sack on her back on the 3D ultrasound. It was 1999 and we lived in a small town. The other machine didn't show it.

It took a lot of phone calls to the insurance company, but eventually I got them to pay for the surgery. We were going to be #47 in the world. There were risks involved. Both of us could die.

Zoe's dad and I had asked our priest to start a little prayer chain for the morning we had surgery scheduled. The day we left I reminded him that it was Friday at 11am. He leaned over and whispered, "Silly girl, we are praying you don't NEED the surgery and you come home."

What??????????????????????????????????????

Never piss off a pregnant woman, especially one carrying a baby with special needs. We were only 24. We were scared shitless. I was not happy.

We had to be there all week for testing and shots to help her lungs develop because most of the babies were also being born premature. Cutting into the uterus at 20 weeks and sewing it back up seemed to trigger early arrival, but she would have her back repaired early enough that the theory was she would not need a shunt. To date, there had been no improvement below the waist as far as mobility or bladder/bowel control, so the reason to do it was to prevent the need for a shunt. Shunt malfunctions were the highest risk of early death for kids with SB, so we moved ahead.

One of the requirements was to meet with a team of medical ethics professionals. The board room table was full. They asked us many questions. We were allowed to pull out at any time. At the end of the 2-hour meeting, they said the only common thread they had found with all the families they had interviewed was faith. Many different religions, all similar beliefs and language, and everyone had put their hand over their heart when they answered, with tear filled eyes;

"We feel called."

"We know God will protect us."

"We are part of something bigger."

"This is part of our mission in life, to take this risk for medical advancement."

It was the first time I saw common thread in different faiths.

It seemed to matter less WHAT you believed, and more THAT you believed…deep in your heart…the words didn't seem to matter as much as the emotion.

I was scheduled for surgery Friday morning. They would take my uterus out, lay it on my stomach, make a small incision, and sew up the hole in her back.

Thursday night we got a call from the neurosurgeon, "I don't know what to say, but the MRI came back without a Chiari malformation (brain tissue is pulled into the spinal canal). We haven't seen this before. All the babies have had it. She still has hydrocephalus (water on the brain), so we don't know whether or not the surgery will improve her chances of not needing a shunt. It is up to you if we proceed."

What??????????????????????????????????????

Ok God, I see what you are doing here.

I said, "She had it when we last had an ultrasound. Are you sure it's not there?"

He said, "An MRI is more precise, so it is more likely she never had one. We aren't sure why the hydrocephalus is so severe without it though. We are perplexed."

Long story short, we did not go through with it. When I got centered, and accessed my HS, I could see a vision of us walking in some type of park pushing a stroller, and Zoe was walking next to us. I made the decision to think, "everything is going to be fine." I have said it thousands of times since. That thought has programmed everything.

I trusted my HS (or intuition). I trusted God (who I believe my HS had a direct connection with). We surrendered. We went home. To this day she does not have a shunt. I did not for one single second believe she would. I also believed fully in her ability to walk.

Beliefs are thoughts we keep thinking. Beliefs matter more than facts or circumstances.

How Do You Control Your Thoughts?

Practice, practice, practice.

Catch the negative ones early.

Have a mantra or positive vision to replace them with.

Stay detached emotionally.

My favorite is "Everything is always working out for me." I was using it when I got pregnant after having surgery to clean out my endometriosis at age 23. He said I had a 50/50 chance to get pregnant within 3 months. After that it went to nearly zero. I said that until I believed it in every cell of my body many times a day. On month 3, we conceived.

I was using that line when the other two events happened as well, but like I've said before, there comes a time with your kids that your belief in them doesn't trump their belief in themselves. That is a whole other level of surrender.

You cannot control other people. If you put "I am so happy now that my husband picks up after himself" on your manifesto, you are likely to be disappointed. Write goals and dreams that only you are in control of, then surrender them and enjoy the journey toward them.

Would you go sailing for a quarter mile? Would you want to get to where you are going at lightning speed, or do you like to enjoy the gentle waves and breeze on the way?

Tony Robbins says "You are not an amount of time away from your manifestation, you are a vibration away."

When you are struggling with your thoughts, focus on doing what makes you feel good. Play cards with your neighbors, see a funny movie, get in the zone by not thinking about the absence of it. Focus on what is going well for you. Enjoy the waves.

9 CONTROLLING YOUR EMOTIONS

"It's so important to realize that every time you get upset, it drains your emotional energy. Losing your cool makes you tired. Getting angry a lot messes with your health."

Joyce Meyer

I listened to Joyce's podcast every day when I was driving my dental outreach van around for a solid year. It made me feel better than the radio did. If I get no other point across in this book I hope you understand that the teachers you listen to, the books you read, the words you write, and the goals you set, mean very little compared to learning how to make yourself FEEL GOOD.

As a people pleasing, Acts of Service woman, making myself feel good felt downright WRONG. Selfish. Shameful…ick.

I judged others who were good at self-soothing, including my now husband. He taught me most of what I know about the phrase, "My cup runneth over (psalm 23:5)." When we don't fill our own cup first, there is nothing left to spill out onto others. You cannot pour from an empty cup. Period. It is literally impossible. Remember the low battery picture? That is where self-care needs to be your priority.

Self-care is not selfish. Practicing self-love is where all change begins.

What do you regularly say to yourself? Is it kind? Is it mean? Does it help or hinder your progress? Does it cause you to feel better or worse? "Kind words are like honey—sweet to the soul and healthy for the body (Proverbs 16:24)."

Have you heard of Masaru Emoto? He is a Japanese author and pseudoscientist who wrote *The Hidden Messages in Water*. He said that human consciousness has an effect on the molecular structure of water. Say nice things, and the molecules are beautiful. Say mean things and they are ugly. Since our bodies are approximately 70% water, doesn't it make sense that positive self-talk may have the same effect on us?

To Change an Emotion, Name It

Esther and Jerry Hicks wrote a book called, *Ask and it Is Given*. In it, are many, many tools for self-development, self-discovery, and self-mastery. Esther channels a group consciousness from the other side that she calls Abraham. I thought it was super weird at first, but the book and Esther's YouTube videos have helped me find and reprogram my outdated loops so much that I cannot write this book without including them.

One of the most helpful tools Abraham has given us is the Emotional Scale. I use it when privately coaching to help people figure out what they are feeling, and where they'd like to be instead.

When you catch yourself having a thought that doesn't feel good, check in with yourself and see where you are on this chart. Don't try to go from jealousy to happiness, that is too far of a stretch.

Anything below 8 is a downward spiral. You will move from frustration to overwhelm, doubt and worry quickly. Anything above 8 is an upward spiral. Hopefulness easily leads to other good feeling emotions.

The Emotional Scale~*Ask and It Is Given* (Esther and Jerry Hicks. pg 114)

1. Joy-Knowledge-Empowerment-Freedom-Love-Appreciation
2. Passion
3. Enthusiasm-Eagerness- Happiness
4. Positive Expectation-Belief
5. Optimism
6. Hopefulness
7. Contentment
8. Boredom
9. Pessimism
10. Frustration-Irritation-Impatience
11. Overwhelm
12. Disappointment
13. Doubt
14. Worry
15. Blame
16. Discouragement
17. Anger
18. Revenge
19. Hatred-Rage
20. Jealousy
21. Insecurity-Guild-Unworthiness
22. Fear-Grief-Depression-Despair-Powerlessness

Boredom (8) is like neutral. When you are in the lower vibes that may be the best you can hope for, to feel nothing. Many people who state they are depressed have a period of time where they struggle to feel anything. It may be the meds they are on, or just that they are climbing the ladder.

Wherever you fall try to move the needle just a little bit and see if you can find a thought that goes with that emotion. For instance, if you feel worried about a test coming up, what thought would go with doubt? That is one higher. "I doubt I'll do well, but you never know!" That feels better than worry doesn't it?

Keep moving up the scale until you can reach neutral. Then shoot for the positive stuff.

If that doesn't work, go all the way into your emotion. They are there for a reason! What is your body trying to tell you? Is there a habit you should consider removing? Chew on it.

You don't swallow your food whole, you have to process it. The same goes for your emotions. You have to move THROUGH them. You won't get anywhere trying to get around them.

Life is full of peaks and valleys. Every time you get to the top of a beautiful mountain you are going to see something you couldn't see from the bottom and say, "I wonder what that is like?" You know you are going to have to go down in the valley again, it's just part of the journey. Don't get stuck there.

Have a friend you can call to help you move forward again. Don't look for someone who will let you complain, or validate how bad your life sucks. Look for people who you look up to for their energy and "get it togetherness."

Hire a coach. It doesn't have to be me, just work with someone. I believe deep down in my bones with 100% certainty that EVERYONE needs a coach, and that EVERYONE gets way more value out of it than what they invest. It changes the way you see and process life. It improves all of your interactions with people. It makes you feel calm, and centered amidst the stormy seas.

If you cannot afford it right now, see if you can find a therapist who also has coach or behavioral therapy training. That often means that they are more future focused. Remember, sitting in therapy talking about your past mistakes and hurt just keeps you in that loop, activating those emotions.

Do whatever it takes to keep your emotions in check. Learn to label them before you attempt to change them.

Feelings are like kids, don't stuff them in the trunk but don't let them drive either.

Remember to continue to watch yourself for times you think or say, "When I have _____, I will feel _____."

I have gotten stuck in that trap so many times, so I am not judging you in any fashion. We are human after all.

I thought I would feel skinny after a hysterectomy, but I gained weight and feel fat.

I thought I would feel an unlimited sense of earning power owning my business, but I miss the steady paycheck.

I thought I would feel a sense of freedom and flexibility working fully from home, but I also feel lonely.

There is dichotomy in all things. All things have good aspects and bad aspects. It's more of a tradeoff.

The cool thing is you get to control what you focus on with your thoughts.

When I catch myself now I just notice. I don't get pulled into the negative emotion, I just say, "Huh, I guess my former situation had some really positive aspects that I missed because I was so focused on what else I wanted instead."

I want to help you find good in all the situations, but you can only do that by noticing the bad too.

YOU HAVE TO FEEL THE FEELING FIRST TO GET THE THING.

10 HOW TO TAKE INSPIRED ACTION

"I have been impressed with the urgency of doing. Knowing is not enough; we must apply. Being willing is not enough; we must do."
Leonardo da Vinci

Another way to say this is that when an inspired idea happens, it will float to another if you don't do anything with it (Liz Gilbert, ***Big Magic***).

Liz says that thoughts float around like dandelion seeds. They move to and fro until someone grabs them. If you let them go, someone else may take hold. If you use them, they are your creation. She supports the theory that we are all connected. One person's passion and execution of an idea may benefit another.

I define inspired action as an idea that seems to come out of nowhere, that makes you feel whole, and excited. I believe you have 24 hours to take ANY small action on that idea for it to "stick" and become reality in your life.

If we use the "water the seeds, pluck the weeds" analogy, you are asking yourself if this is something you want to grow in your garden. If not, you pluck it, and it floats over to your neighbor's garden.

Inspired Action is action that feels REALLY, REALLY GOOD.

You know because you wake up excited to do it, or you can't fall asleep because you are doing it until you are exhausted.

I wrote the bulk of this book in days, but I had been writing it in my head, and with my clients and experiences, for at least 5 years. It took me a few weeks to edit and finish it, but once I made the decision to do it, it poured out. I had to detach from the outcome to get it done. I had to commit to taking Massive Imperfect Action to see the next step on the staircase. The title and purpose I started with changed over and over as I typed. What I wanted to say got more and more clear with each day that went by. Doing helped me gain clarity more than thinking ever could. I had to be willing to suck, and do it anyway. It had to be because I liked to write, not because I was going to be a best seller. The journey had to matter more than the destination.

I got SO INSPIRED, that I forgot to eat and could not sleep. On the first day of spring, I could not stop writing. Growth feels good to me. I've been self-coaching long enough that I've gotten comfortable being uncomfortable.

Inspired Action is anything that comes up for you after centering. If it seems to come out of nowhere, or doesn't even seem like an idea you would normally have, try it out and see what happens. Often, it is just a stepping stone to the next thing that WILL matter.

Examples:

"Maybe you should try the other grocery store tonight" and a friend you haven't seen in years is there.

"McDonalds's doesn't sound appetizing" and you come home to

your hubby making dinner.

"Maybe I should quit. I can temp and make more money for less drama." So, you do, and have never been happier.

"What if you just forgave him?" So, you do, and everything good blossoms from there.

Inspired Action is any action that feels out of the norm or stretched beyond your abilities at first glance, but then seems like the appropriate next step after you look at it from your HS perspective.

It will feel good when you do it. You may not have any idea where it came from or why you thought or felt it. That is your HS whispering to you. He or she knows what you don't. They can see the larger perspective.

Go into your Wellness Room and get centered. See what comes up.

My Most Powerful Coaching Question

Another way of coming up with the "next step" is to ask yourself this powerful question:

"On a scale of 1 to 10, with 10 being highest, how satisfied am I with my life overall right now?"

The first number that shows up in your brain is correct. Intuition (HS) only takes 1-2 seconds. Doubt, fear, and SC will want you to think about it until you forget that you were wondering and move on to something else. That is how you to stay programmed, and "safe."

Sometimes people get really overwhelmed and sad with how low their number is, but the good news is that by consciously knowing where you are, you can decide where you'd like to be instead.

I am a 10. When I first started self-coaching I was a 4 or 5. My SC was writing my story, not my HS. I had to let my heart take over.

Let's say you are a 6. I would ask you what it would take for you to be an 8? Your next step lives somewhere in that answer.

Example:

Me "What would it take for you to say you are an 8?"

Client "I don't know. Maybe to have a different job?"

Me "Ok, what would someone who has this different job be believing about themselves or the world around them?"

Client "Maybe that it was easy to find work?"

Me "Yes, that makes sense. Do you believe it is easy to find work?"

Client "No, I have been telling everyone that it is hard to find work since I lost my job…I heard it on the news. I had no idea how much it was holding me back from being serious about my job search."

Me "What is your ideal job?"

Client lists everything…

Me "Do you believe it is possible for you to find a job like that with your current degree, background, skill set, location, and network?"

Client "No."

Me "Can you see how your thoughts are limiting you more than the facts?"

Client "I guess…yeah, I see that now."

Me "So what would you like to be true?"

Client "That it is easy to find my ideal job."

Me "That is your mantra this week. Say it over and over until a smile comes to your face—that means you believe it."

Client "It is easy to find my ideal job. I already feel better just saying it!"

Me "Awesome, that means your mind is accepting the new programming. You got this! I am excited for you! What is your next step then?"

Client "To reach out to my old boss and tell him I am willing to come back, but these are the changes I desire."

Me "Great, that is your homework. Text me when it's complete and let me know the outcome. I can't wait to talk to you next week!"

The following week the client was still at the same job with all the new desires in place. Her life satisfaction number was a 9. I had coached her for one month, and we had put a lot of past stuff away. During the 3rd month we were able to focus on the rest of the "instruments" from my symphony analogy: health, marriage, fun.

It wasn't the job that was the problem, it was her thoughts. She didn't enjoy work because she didn't have enough responsibility or creative control and she would get lost in her head about the past while doing menial tasks. Once she gained control of her mind, and got clear on her ideal job setting, she was brave enough to ask for what she wanted. She went from being reactive to proactive. She took control of her own happiness instead of waiting for it to show up in her life like some hero riding a white horse. She realized she was the hero of her own story and the only one who could save her.

Self-Coaching Mastery Recap:

1. Dive in shallow water first—deal with the day to day stuff for practice

2. Do a deep dive into the past—look for where the tie still binds and is holding you back

3. Redirect the sails using gratitude—start with the basics until you

can find appreciation for everything you have, and everything on its way to you, with ease

4.   Enjoy the ride—Once you realize your thoughts were the problem, not your circumstances, you find freedom and joy in every day

11. What to do when you get stuck

"We are set in our ways, bound by our
perspectives and stuck in our thinking."
Joel Osteen

No matter how long you have been on this journey, there will come a time you think about turning back. The fear is completely normal. It means your SC is working!

I am already thinking about adjusting my sails. I am 11 Chapters in! If you haven't embarked on your journey yet, it seems easier to just not go, which is why I am a believer in massive imperfect action. If we wait until we feel ready we will never act.

There are some things you can only learn BY DOING.

There are some things you will only learn BY FAILING.

Will Smith says, "Fail forward."

When you spend more time thinking than acting, you leave room for doubt. You leave space for what others think. You allow your SC to support the narrative of failure. The longer you give it, the more proof it will dig up from your past to support it. The more it will trigger you so that you act in a manner that is consistent with failure.

Remember that Reticular Activating System we discussed? It's job is to filter. Your job is to *program* the filter. The RAS is your brain. Your higher self is your heart. Your HS is the best programmer there is. He or she does not experience the fear that your SC has on speed dial. You win the battle within by getting your brain and heart to work together for your common good. You have to be a deliberate creator. You have to get good at making decisions. You have to get comfortable being uncomfortable.

When you second guess yourself, that is called resistance. People experience it at different stages of change. My sister hits it in the beginning, so once she makes it past, it's smooth sailing. I hit it at the end, right before I share it with the world. I have complete blog articles, presentations, and videos that I bailed on AFTER completion. Learning what resistance feels like, and where you normally hit it will help you overcome it.

Resistance can feel like hitting shallow water with your sailboat. You can sit there, or you can ask another sailor to help push you your boat off the sand bar.

Now that you've learned my methods, and hopefully had a chat with your HS, you should be realizing that you never sail alone.

YOU can be your own coach.

I was my very first client. I could not be an effective coach for others until I dealt with my own stuff, and learned how to manage it.

I am now known nationally, have a successful coaching business, and have started a nonprofit. I have an amazing, supportive husband and gifted daughters and step-sons who teach me new perspectives all the time. To the outside world, my life is perfect.

But inside my world is STILL fraught with angst. The negative thoughts don't necessarily go away, I just learned how to turn down the volume.

"What if no one buys it"

"You're not good enough"

"They are all gonna laugh at you" (said with the voice of the mom from the movie *Carrie*)

Thanks to self-coaching, I know how to pluck those weeds and redirect my sails. I am launching this series imperfectly, because it is the only way I ever finish anything. Expect some typos. Expect some of my ramblings to leave you confused. Look for what you like. Find the nugget that speaks to you. I usually remember only one or two small things from each book I read, and that is my hope for you with this book.

We never know someone's thoughts unless we live in there with them. Every mind is scary. Everyone suffers, unless they take control.

I am sorry friend, but you will get stuck. You will fail. You will suffer. The sea of life offers all the experiences. You get to choose what to focus on. Free will is dichotomous.

I have raised a special needs daughter, and been a single mom through two divorces, bankruptcy, and foreclosure. I nearly lost my fiancé in a bad motorcycle accident. I had a suicidal/depressed daughter at the same time we lost my step-son to suicide, which has broken our hearts wide open. I kind of lost his dad that day too. The emotional weight of losing a child, especially in that way, causes a hole in your soul that can never be filled.

I know grief.

I know loss.

I know those bottom-feeder emotions well.

I have risen above.

My family has risen above.

If we can rise from the rubble, you can too. Stop laying beneath it. Use the fallen debris of your past dreams as stepping stones toward the top. Your higher self will be waiting.

It is not too late to rewrite your story. Suffering is optional. I am honored to help you gain mastery over your life. I believe in your healing and all the possibility buried deep within. I know you have great gifts to share with the world. Let's unwrap them together.

Go to https://jamiedooley.com to take the next step toward creating a life you love.

ABOUT THE AUTHOR

Jamie Dooley is certified life coach, as well as an author, speaker, and written goal setting expert. She has coached hundreds of people individually, and is nationally recognized as a change agent and thought leader. She also has a certification program *Called to Coach*. To explore working with her, go to https://jamiedooley.com/contact, or email info@jamiedooley.com.

Look for her free Facebook group "Self-Coaching Mastery" where these topics and future topics from the series will be covered.

Facebook business page Jamie Dooley Coaching (@jamieismycoach)
Instagram jamieismycoach

Learn more about her current offerings or read client testimonials at www.jamiedooley.com